Alamo to Espada

A Vintage Postcard Profile of
San Antonio's Spanish Missions

One February about 1910, a postcard photographer at
San José Mission snapped these tourists, one of whom
wrote on the back of the card, "We had a fine time that
day, but it was cold as the mischief."

# Alamo to Espada

*A Vintage Postcard Profile of*

*San Antonio' s Spanish Missions*

Lewis F. Fisher

Maverick Publishing Company

MAVERICK PUBLISHING COMPANY
P.O. Box 6355, San Antonio, Texas 78209

ALSO BY LEWIS F. FISHER

*Saving San Antonio: The Precarious Preservation of a Heritage*
*Crown Jewel of Texas: The Story of San Antonio's River*
*San Antonio: Outpost of Empires*
*The Spanish Missions of San Antonio*
*Eyes Right! A Vintage Postcard Profile of San Antonio's Military*

Library of Congress Cataloging-in-Publication Data

Fisher, Lewis F.
    Alamo to Espada : a vintage postcard profile of San Antonio's
Spanish missions / Lewis F. Fisher.
      p. cm.
    ISBN 1-893271-15-3 (softcover : alk. paper)
    1. Alamo (San Antonio, Tex.)–History–Pictorial works.  2. Spanish
mission buildings–Texas–San Antonio–History–Pictorial works.  3. San
Antonio (Tex.)–History–Pictorial works.  4. San Antonio (Tex.)–
Buildings, structures, etc.–Pictorial works.  5. Church architecture–
Texas–San Antonio–Pictorial works.  6. Postcards–Texas–San Antonio.
7. Missions, Spanish–Texas–San Antonio–History–Pictorial works.
I. Title.
F394.S2118 A433 2001
976.4'351–dc21

                                                          2001016418

11 10 09 07 06 05 04 03 02 01     10 9 8 7 6 5 4 3 2 1

Printed in the United States of America on acid-free paper

ABBREVIATIONS IN CAPTIONS:  Postcard publishers' names, when
known, appear in italics at the end of each description. "n.p." stands
for no publisher identified, "pm." for postmarked.

# Contents

San Antonio's Spanish missions were popular illustrations as soon as picture postcards began appearing, like this one, in the late 1890s. *(Paul Wagner, San Antonio)*

Photography techniques had improved by the 1920s, and the missions—particularly the Alamo—remained favorite subjects for evoking memories of San Antonio. *(n.p.)*

# Introduction

Postcard publishers rushed into San Antonio at the beginning of the twentieth century to sell the new medium to the hordes of travelers coming to the picturesque city.

San Antonio, the largest city in Texas, even then was widely known as one of America's most colorful places. Authentic remnants of Spanish colonial times were within walking distance of new hotels, along narrow streets recalling the city's past as an isolated frontier town. Tourists eagerly picked from the burgeoning variety of picture postcards and mailed them by the thousands to friends and family. In the process, quickly evolving scenes were documented, change by change.

One perennial San Antonio attraction has been the city's five Spanish missions, the largest such cluster in the United States. All were established in San Antonio—postcard captions to the contrary—from 1718 to 1731, as Spain sought to transform Native Americans into European-style settlers, who would establish new towns  throughout the empty frontier and be a buffer between the threatening French in Louisiana and New Spain's silver mines in northern Mexico.

Today, one former mission is preserved as the Alamo while the others, largely restored, make up San Antonio Missions National Historical Park. Not long ago all five were in ruins, in danger of disappearing altogether.

*Alamo to Espada* portrays this transformation through vintage postcards printed from the very end of the nineteenth century through the first half of the twentieth. The Alamo evolves from a battle-scarred shell into its modern-day form, a shrine sustained by a sometimes mythic remembrance. Concepción's barnyard surroundings are cleaned up. San José changes from a crumbling church and granary back to a full-scale walled complex. San Juan and Espada likewise are pulled from the brink.

The impact of the missions goes far beyond the confines of the mission compounds. The revival of mission architecture in California in the 1890s found a ready welcome in San Antonio, where postcards, approaching the height of their popularity, began recording new Mission Revival structures from railroad stations to funeral homes, many adopting elements of the Alamo. As Mission/Alamo Revival evolved into Spanish Colonial Revival, these new landmarks, too, turned up on postcards.

As the physical face of San Antonio changed, so did the appearance of postcards themselves. At first, Post Office Department regulations specified that messages be written only on the front, requiring space to be left around illustrations for handwriting. Then messages were permitted beside addresses on the back, allowing images to take up the entire front. Cardstock photographic paper freed photographers to produce custom-made "real photo" postcards.

Color lithography techniques developed in Germany fueled the "golden era" of postcards, which extended until World War I ended the export of German-made cards. By then cards folded in envelopes were taking over the greeting function of postcards, and improved telephone communication was replacing some uses of the written word. Still, postcards remained popular, trending toward white borders in the 1920s, linen-type surfaces in the 1930s and present-day glossy surfaces in the 1950s.

Some of the most appealing early postcards are those of London's Raphael Tuck & Sons, which, as noted on the back, enjoyed the status of "Art Publishers to their Majesties the King and Queen." Tuck's typical early photochrome images, printed in Germany, had a feathered lower border that left room for a handwritten message. Tuck's San Antonio missions series, which illustrates the first pages of five *Alamo to Espada* chapters, is enhanced by the superimposing of images of well-dressed tourists. Otherwise lonesome scenes thus gain an Edwardian elegance, as in the particularly charming "carriage excursion" on Tuck's view of Mission Espada.

Gratitude for sharing their postcard collections with readers goes to Robin Ellis, Frank Thompson, Raymond D. White, San Antonio's Witte Museum and to L. B. Griffith Jr. for access to the collection of his mother, the late Ilse Griffith.

# 1. Mission San Antonio de Valero— The Alamo

Established in 1718 with the founding of San Antonio itself, Mission San Antonio de Valero moved twice. About 1724 the mission reached its third and final location, above a bend in the San Antonio River a short distance across from the civilian settlement. There, 20 years later, work began on a permanent church, still unfinished when the mission closed in 1795.

In the chaos following Mexico's independence from Spain, the compound—by then known as the Alamo—became a refuge for the town's defenders. A band of some 187 Texas revolutionaries barricaded within was annhilated in 1836 by a 5,000-man army under General Antonio López de Santa Anna.

Although the Catholic Church sold the rest of the complex to others when the Army closed its Alamo supply depot, in 1883 the state bought the Alamo church as a memorial. The "Second Battle of the Alamo" began in 1903, when Daughters of the Republic of Texas sought to enlarge the shrine. Property purchases were completed by 1936, when the complex appeared much as it does today.

SAN ANTONIO, Tex. The Alamo · Built 1718

Am 6. Maerz 1836 wurde dieses Gebaeude und die damit verbundene Festung von 4000 Mexikanern belagert. Die ganze, aus 181 tapferen Texanern bestehende Besatzung kam bei der Verteidigung der Festung um's Leben.

To promote postcard sales among San Antonio's large German-born community, at the beginning of the twentieth century a German-language caption describing the Battle of the Alamo was overprinted on this popular card. (*Raphael Tuck & Sons, London*)

THE FALL OF THE ALAMO    SAN ANTONIO, TEXAS

Remains of the Alamo's mission walls and outbuildings can be seen in this card of the 1836 Battle of the Alamo, printed to promote travel to San Antonio on the Southern Pacific Railroad's Sunset Route through the Southwest. *(Interstate Co., Chicago)*

SIEGE OF THE ALAMO MARCH 6TH, 1836

This imaginary view of the Battle of the Alamo has a Lone Star flag flying high over a gabled parapet not yet built atop the old mission church, plus further enhancements like non-existent second story side windows for sharpshooters. *(n.p.)*

Fury over loss of the Alamo garrison helped spur Texas revolutionaries to defeat Mexican General Santa Anna the next month at San Jacinto, where Texas General Sam Houston, wounded above his right ankle, received the surrender. *(Nic Tengg, San Antonio)*

The Alamo, The Cradle of Texas Liberty, San Antonio, Texas.

Although the old Alamo church, leased as an Army depot and then a grocery warehouse, was bought by the state in 1883, adjacent property was owned by others, and various buildings began to crowd the landmark. *(S. Langsdorf & Co., New York)*

Seventy years after the battle, much of the old mission plaza had become the fashionable commercial Alamo Plaza, criscrossed by streetcars and carriages and surrounded by buildings in the latest styles. *(George M. Bearce, San Antonio)*

Sensing that its military history was good for business, the mercantile firm of Hugo & Schmeltzer built military-style ramparts around remains of the mission convento. The Federal Building is at the rear, the Maverick Bank at the left. *(Nic Tengg, San Antonio)*

Blooming Spanish daggers common in the dry stretches of West Texas were being promoted as palm trees as landscaping on Alamo Plaza evolved. *(Paul Ebers, San Antonio, pm. 1910)*

Early tourists found the onetime mission church, operated as a museum first by the City of San Antonio and then by the Daughters of the Republic of Texas, to be an irresistable spot for personalized photographic postcards to send home. *(n.p.)*

The home built by the Gallagher family behind the Alamo can be glimpsed at the far right of this postcard view mailed to Springfield, Illinois two days after Christmas 1905. *(Nic Tengg, San Antonio, pm. 1905)*

Removal of part of the wooden framework around the old mission convento, left, revealed a lower two-story structure, as cars and tour buses parked nearby. *(Dahrooge Co., San Antonio)*

The wintertime chill in the stone interior of the Alamo was alleviated by a woodburning stove, as indicated by the smokestack visible on the south side of the building at right. *(Nic Tengg, San Antonio, pm. 1908)*

This Fiesta parade float promoted Daughters of the Republic of Texas fundraising in 1903–05 to purchase the convento property adjoining the Alamo. It was printed in an "oilette" format to resemble an oil painting. *(Raphael Tuck & Sons, London)*

This view toward the front in the Alamo church's early days as a museum shows the frame roof dating from the structure's use as a quartermaster depot for the U.S. Army. *(Grombach-Faisans Co., New Orleans)*

The beginnings of the Alamo's collection of Texas relics line the walls in this view toward the rear of the building, its roof never completed by Spanish missionaries. *(Nic Tengg, San Antonio)*

A new support frame displays this cannon, apparently one of the several unearthed on or near the original Alamo compound. *(n.p.)*

An American and a Texas flag were added to this view of the Alamo church's interior looking in from the front door. *(Nic Tengg, San Antonio)*

A 165-foot monument enclosing an elevator rising to a balcony overlooking the Alamo was first planned in 1887, but fundraising was unsuccessful. *(H.H.T. Co.)*

## THE DESIGN OF THE ALAMO MONUMENT

### BY ALFRED GILES, SAN ANTONIO, TEXAS

Architect Alfred Giles promoted this plan for a park that would replace the old mission convento building beside the Alamo with green space to be in front of a new hotel, with the Alamo church remaining as a shrine to Texas liberty. The hotel was never built. *(n.p.)*

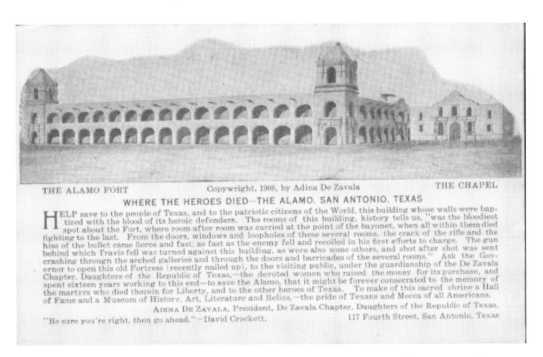

THE ALAMO FORT      Copywright, 1908, by Adina De Zavala      THE CHAPEL

### WHERE THE HEROES DIED—THE ALAMO, SAN ANTONIO, TEXAS

HELP save to the people of Texas, and to the patriotic citizens of the World, this building whose walls were baptized with the blood of its heroic defenders. The rooms of this building, history tells us, "was the bloodiest spot about the Fort, where room after room was carried at the point of the bayonet, when all within them died fighting to the last. From the doors, windows and loopholes of these several rooms, the crack of the rifle and the hiss of the bullet came fierce and fast; as fast as the enemy fell and recoiled in his first efforts to charge. The gun behind which Travis fell was turned against this building, as were also some others, and shot after shot was sent crashing through the arched galleries and through the doors and barricades of the several rooms." Ask the Governor to open this old Fortress (recently nailed up), to the visiting public, under the guardianship of the De Zavala Chapter, Daughters of the Republic of Texas,—the devoted women who raised the money for its purchase, and spent sixteen years working to this end—to save the Alamo, that it might be forever consecrated to the memory of the martyrs who died therein for Liberty, and to the other heroes of Texas. To make of this sacred shrine a Hall of Fame and a Museum of History, Art, Literature and Relics,—the pride of Texans and Mecca of all Americans.

ADINA DE ZAVALA, President, De Zavala Chapter, Daughters of the Republic of Texas.

"Be sure you're right, then go ahead."—David Crockett.      117 Fourth Street, San Antonio, Texas

Pioneer preservationist Adina De Zavala was successful in keeping the convento from being torn down altogether for a park, though it did not become a Texas Hall of Fame as she envisioned here, and its second story was removed. *(Adina De Zavala, San Antonio, 1908)*

*Alamo, San Antonio, Texas.*

After a bitter fight between two factions of the Daughters of the Republic of Texas, remains of the old mission convento were gutted and its second story level later removed so the building would not appear to overshadow the old Alamo church. *(n.p., pm. 1913)*

*The Alamo and Fort and Menger Hotel, San Antonio, Tex.*

This view southeast from the Post Office building toward remains of the old Alamo convento "is just as it looks today," wrote the sender of this postcard in 1913. *(H. Budow, San Antonio, pm. 1913)*

The State of Texas repaid Daughters of the Republic of Texas backer Clara Driscoll for her purchase of the Alamo's old mission convento, took title to the property and then entrusted its care and that of the church to the Daughters. *(Acmegraph Co., Chicago)*

San Antonio's turreted Richardson Romanesque Federal Building and Post Office, built in 1890, dominated the northern end of Alamo Plaza. *(n.p.)*

By the 1920s remaining one-story walls of the Alamo's old adjacent building were draped with ivy, while on the opposite side a two-story brick commercial building had arisen. *(Nic Tengg, San Antonio)*

Stones from the Alamo convento's second story formed the rear wall of a newly-trellised arcade while flowers in the shape of a Texas Lone Star were the centerpiece of a nearby garden. *(Nic Tengg, San Antonio)*

Published by The Dahrooge Co., Inc.

A highrise sign advertising Alamo Bottled Beer, "the best beer brewed," was visible from the Alamo complex's new inner courtyard north of the old church. *(Albertype Co., Brooklyn)*

27  NEW ALAMO PARK, ADJOINING THE ALAMO, SAN ANTONIO, TEXAS

A square memorial fountain was built in the 1930s on the site of one of the commercial buildings that stood south of the Alamo church. *(Curt Teich & Co., Chicago, pm. 1936)*

The Alamo and Courtyard, San Antonio, Texas

A printed message on the back of this postcard showing the courtyard's new iron gates boosted San Antonio as "Home of the Alamo, Gulf Breezes and Sunshine." *(San Antonio Card Co., San Antonio)*

A distribution depot for United States Tires was one of two commercial buildings beside the Alamo, its tourist popularity attested by the open-air tour buses parked nearby. *(Albertype Co., Brooklyn)*

By the 1930s, the buildings adjacent to the Alamo on the south had been purchased and replaced with palm trees and a contemplative arched walkway. *(E. C. Kropp Co. Milwaukee)*

An encircling of the Alamo more gradual than that of
1836 seemed complete with the high-rise Medical Arts
Building (1928) and a new Federal Building (1937) to its
left plus occasional use of the lawn for parking. *(n.p.)*

A new enclosure around the Alamo well was built in the courtyard in the 1930s, though postcard captions continued to garble the date of the mission's establishment at that site (about 1724, not 1718). *(n.p.)*

Lights hanging from cedar crossbeams adorned the stone arcade built in the 1930s on the site of commercial buildings that once stood south of the Alamo church. *(n.p.)*

Once the state completed land purchase around the Alamo in 1936, existing buildings were cleared away and two new ones built, including the museum and gift shop above. The new, columned Federal building is right of center. *(Albertype Co., Brooklyn)*

On the opposite side of the Alamo church from the new museum building was built an assembly room and library named Alamo Hall. *(Albertype Co., Brooklyn)*

Near Alamo Hall, the square memorial fountain area was landscaped with native plantings. *(Albertype Co., Brooklyn)*

Remains of the Alamo mission's water supply, the old Spanish *acequia* or ditch, were uncovered and rebuilt during landscaping of the shrine's enlarged grounds in 1936. *(Albertype Co., Brooklyn)*

A cenotaph—an empty monument honoring the dead whose bodies are elsewhere—was designed by sculptor Pompeo Coppini and dedicated on Alamo Plaza in 1940. (*Albertype Co., Brooklyn*)

By the 1940s the restored Alamo church looked virtually the same as at present, with the Texas Lone Star flag flying above. (*n.p.*)

# 2. Remember the Alamo!

The heroism of the Alamo's defenders in the face of overwhelming odds has been an inspiration ever since its fall on March 6, 1836. Sentiment surrounding the event has transcended the physical to the point that visitors expecting to find a restored battle-scarred fortress discover instead a neatly-kept shrine. Its focal point is recognizable as the old mission church, now roofed and air conditioned. Those entering are asked to take no pictures. Men are advised to remove their hats. Outside are contemplative gardens among a few low buildings and discreet signage.

The Alamo church with its gabled parapet is an internationally-revered landmark. Whether one is a military hero, national dignitary, foreign monarch or regular tourist, no visit to San Antonio—or Texas—is complete without a stop and perhaps a speech at the Alamo. The Alamo's wide variety of uses, from patriotic to political to, inevitably, commercial gain, is uniquely revealed in these postcard images.

Even cigar manufacturers have sought immortality in the Alamo's shadow. In about 1912 the initial delivery of Don Juarez Cigars (37,600 of them) was unabashedly trucked in front of the shrine to be photographed for postcard advertising. (*n.p.*)

The Alamo's central role in Texas liberty is symbolized in this patriotic postcard, which shows a surrounding host of Texas images from flags to the state flower, the Bluebonnet. *(W. R. Elliott, Chestertown, Md., 1913)*

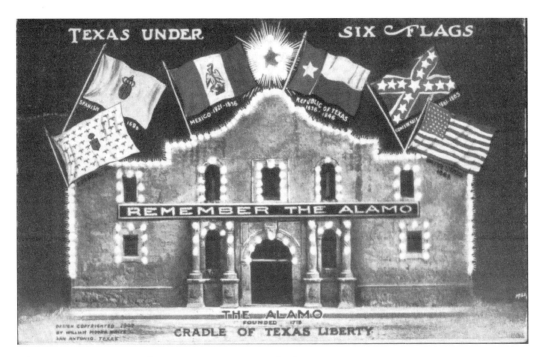

The popular image of the six national flags which once flew over Texas—France, Spain, Mexico, Republic of Texas, Confederacy and United States—was soon linked to the state's most memorable landmark, the Alamo. (*J. R. Wood Co., San Antonio, 1907*)

In their rush to sell postcards, manufacturers came up with a card associating all six flags with "the staff at the Alamo," even though French influence was limited to the Texas coast and the original Alamo may have had no flagstaff. (*A. F. Dahrooge, San Antonio, 1912*)

Annual ceremonies and parades, like this one making the obligatory pass by the Alamo about 1905, are among the numerous remembrances that still keep the Alamo memorialized as a symbol of the fight for freedom. *(n.p.)*

Electricity offered the opportunity to adorn the Alamo for nighttime parades with strings of lights, some forming the Texas Star. *(n.p., pm. 1911)*

Garlands once festooned the Alamo during San Antonio's annual Fiesta, which in the annual Battle of Flowers parade celebrates an outcome of the Alamo defeat, the Texan victory at San Jacinto near present-day Houston. *(H. Budow, San Antonio, 1911)*

Horsedrawn floats pass the Alamo about 1910, about to begin their early practice of circling on Alamo Plaza while occupants threw flowers at each other in a peaceful remembrance of the Battle of San Jacinto. *(H. Budow, San Antonio)*

The Alamo has long been a familiar milestone at which visiting celebrities and even ox teams—this one came through in 1911—can stop and have their arrival recorded. *(n.p.)*

The Alamo made a natural spot for civic leaders to stage this publicity "holdup" to promote a $25,000 fundraising drive for advertising San Antonio nationally, a financial goal reached in two weeks. *(Paul Ebers, San Antonio, pm. 1910)*

Heroism displayed by the Alamo heroes has made the Alamo an opportune stop for public figures visiting Texas. Here President Theodore Roosevelt fills Alamo Plaza in 1905. *(Grombach-Faisans Co., New Orleans)*

President Franklin D. Roosevelt continued the tradition of paying homage to the Alamo heroes during his visit in the Texas Centennial year of 1936. *(n.p.)*

In history-challenged Dallas, the *Dallas Morning News* imported tradition from San Antonio by building this half-scale replica of the Alamo church on the State Fair grounds in Dallas. *(n.p., pm. 1909)*

When Dallas was picked as the site for the Texas Centennial Exposition of 1936, the Alamo replica was moved to the southeast corner of the Exposition grounds and enlarged beside a courtyard featuring the Six Flags. *(Centennial Exposition, Dallas, pm. 1936)*

During the Texas Centennial, San Antonio postcards reminded the world where the real Alamo stood, with the Six Flags superimposed atop its walls. *(Weiner News Co., San Antonio)*

An annual Fiesta event remains a pilgrimage to the Alamo and floral tribute sponsored by the Daughters of the Republic of Texas on the anniversary of the Texan victory at San Jacinto. This pilgrimage filled the seats in front of the Alamo in 1947. *(n.p., pm. 1947)*

In an apparent effort to outdo other Alamo postcard makers by selling sexier cards, this one added "Alamo girls" to the scene, boosting San Antonio on the reverse as being "not only famous with its Alamo but also with girls." *(H. Budow, San Antonio, pm. 1915)*

*A star of hope,*
*A flowerlet blue,*
*And greetings from*
*A Texan true.*

"BLUE BONNET"
TEXAS STATE FLOWER

Foreshadowing sentimental greeting cards printed separately, folded and mailed in envelopes, this postcard purports to bear the image of a "blue bonnet" that actually appears more like a thistle. *(n.p., 1908)*

In seeking to profit from the Alamo's appeal, one unidentified publisher took an old structure several miles away that had an unexciting identification in this postcard . . . *(Dahrooge Co., San Antonio)*

. . . and decided that a lot more cards could be sold if the building's origins were instead fabricated as having been "Davy Crockett's cabin." *(n.p.)*

At least one San Antonio photographer saw the appeal of a painted Alamo backdrop for studio portraits. Posing in 1920 for this photo postcard were Louis Baquera and Claude Cisneros. *(n.p.)*

San Antonio's Badden Produce Co. stamped its name on the back of this greeting card and mailed it to a customer. *(Dahrooge Co., pm. 1914)*

The familiar outline of the Alamo's facade was used as a template for an early roadway chain that began to grow in the 1930s. *(Bone-Crow Co., Waco)*

*Remembrance Advertising*

Serves Your Customer and by
That Service Reminds Him of You

BROWN & BIGELOW SAINT PAUL
MINNESOTA

(OVER)

This postcard printed by a Minnesota calendar firm to acknowledge orders was designed with a hole punched at the top so it, too, could be hung as a reminder. *(Brown & Bigelow, St. Paul, pm. 1940)*

# 3. Mission Nuestra Señora de la Purísima Concepción de Acuña

After San Antonio's remaining Spanish missions closed in 1824, memories of their names—to say nothing of the spelling—began to fade. Until mission restoration began in the early twentieth century, the outlying missions were known mainly by their order in distance from downtown San Antonio. Thus Mission Concepción became "The First Mission."

Founded in 1716 and moved from East Texas to the banks of the San Antonio River in 1731, "The First Mission" for several years was headquarters for all of its order's Texas missions. The Father President's office remains on the convento's surviving second floor.

Mission Concepción's twin-towered stone church was dedicated in 1755, and is the oldest unreconstructed Spanish church in the nation. Although the adjoining convento was once used for housing farm animals and storage, some of the original interior fresco work painted by Native American converts survived and has been restored by an international team of art conservators.

SAN ANTONIO, Mission Conception (The First Mission).

Original structures adjoining the twin-towered Spanish church of Mission Concepción were converted into living quarters and farm buildings before the complex's final restoration. *(Raphael Tuck & Sons, London)*

7 – First Mission, San Antonio, Texas.

Mission Concepción's church was not only closest to San Antonio of the four outlying missions, it was also the best preserved, encouraging the Catholic Church, starting in 1861, to periodically refurbish the interior for services. *(Saul Wolfson Co.)*

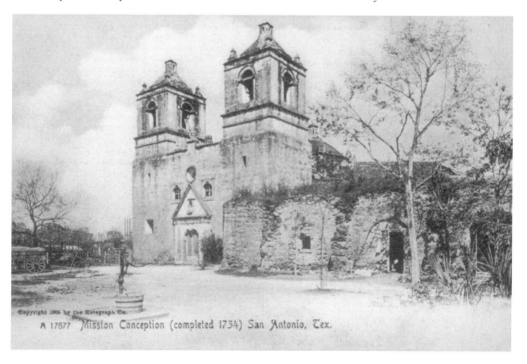

Copyright 1905 by the Rotograph Co.
A 17677   Mission Conception (completed 1734) San Antonio, Tex.

A hand-powered water pump was installed over the original well of the mission, its lands leased by the Catholic Church to farmers, whose wagons can be seen at the far left. *(Rotograph Co., New York, 1905)*

Board fences once kept farm animals close to remains of Mission Concepción's original outbuildings. *(Nic Tengg, San Antonio, pm. 1907)*

By 1910 farm use of the mission church area had ceased, the old convento was reroofed and side windows were cut into doors for use of resident priests. *(Albertype Co., Brooklyn)*

The old hand pump at the mission well had been replaced with a more picturesque enclosure with a hand-drawn bucket by the time this greeting card was sent in 1915. (n.p., pm. 1915)

Longtime San Antonio stationer and postcard publisher Nic Tengg added an interior view to this card showing a tidied-up Concepción church. (Nic Tengg, San Antonio.)

A mural painted on the chancel walls in 1887 to reflect the mission church's dedication at the time to Our Lady of Lourdes was removed during another redecoration, in 1913. *(n.p.)*

Ancient Baptismal font of Azteg coroing, in Mission Concepcion. San Antonio, Texas.

Irregular placement of the baptismal font suggests it was a late arrival to the baptistry, perhaps moved from the Alamo—which has similar sculptural detail—after that mission closed. (*Grombach-Faisans Co., New Orleans*)

Old stone steps, in Mission Concepcion. San Antonio, Texas.

This crumbling stone convento stairway, since repaired, leads to the second-floor office of the Spanish priest who supervised his order's missions in Texas. *(Grombach-Faisans Co., New Orleans)*

As tourism to the missions increased, wire fencing and swinging gates replaced the old board fence along the county road that until recent years passed directly in front of the Concepción church. *(Nic Tengg, San Antonio, pm. 1920)*

A JOY RIDE AT FIRST MISSION.     SAN ANTONIO, TEXAS.

Published by The Dahrooge Co., Inc.

An Army truck doubled as a tour bus for this World War I-era group of soldiers, among the many stationed in San Antonio. *(Dahrooge Co., San Antonio)*

# 4. Mission San José y San Miguel de Aguayo

Mission San José, the second in distance from downtown San Antonio, has been known as the "Queen of the Missions of New Spain." Founded along the San Antonio River by the venerable missionary Father Antonio Margil de Jesús in 1720, the baroque carvings on its facade and sacristy window are considered among the finest Spanish colonial sculpture in North America. Despite frequent epidemics, 350 Native American converts were living there in 1768.

Even as San José's fame as a travel destination grew in the nineteenth century, the compound's walls disappeared for building materials and the granary's roof fell in. Even the church, its dome having collapsed in 1874, seemed on its way out when preservationists made their first halting efforts at repairs in 1902.

But, as the postcard images on the following pages illustrate, the church was gradually put back together, the granary, perimeter walls and Indian barracks were rebuilt and even the small mission mill was reconstructed.

This view of the church of Mission San José, largest and most successful Spanish mission in Texas, shows the work of early preservationists, who patched cracks on the tower and put up a wire fence to keep farm animals out. *(Raphael Tuck & Sons, London, pm. 1914)*

Early postcards of Mission San José's church show it fenced from remains of the courtyard surrounding it, with undergrowth obscuring the entrance. *(J. W. Hutchison, San Antonio.)*

The collapse of San José's northern and eastern walls, roof and dome left only a partial shell of the once-proud mission church, shown in this postcard printed when messages were not permitted on the address side. *(McLean & Mudge, San Antonio, pm. 1906)*

Public roads criscrossed the former mission plaza, its walls long before scavanged for building materials, in this side view showing the extent of the mission church and onetime convento. *(Joske Bros., San Antonio, pm. 1909)*

San José's church facade is more visible in this view, apparently made in winter when there was little foliage. The domed sacristy adjoins the church at the right, in front of the arches. *(Nic Tengg, San Antonio)*

Other than the church, San José's only original surviving building was its nearby stone granary, its exterior wall having also served as part of the mission's perimeter defense wall. *(J. W. Hutchison, San Antonio)*

New tour companies offered affluent tourists arriving in San Antonio by rail the option of renting automobiles and uniformed drivers for the trek, sometimes over muddy roads, to the missions. *(n.p.)*

SOUTH WINDOW OF BAPTISTRY, MISSION SAN JOSÉ.

AT SAN ANTONIO, TEXAS

A patterned weaving drapes the inside of the sacristy's elaborately carved window, later called the "Rose Window," often termed the finest example of Spanish colonial sculpture in the United States. *(n.p.)*

Entrance to the three-domed sacristy, completed in 1777, was through this carved entrance the rear of the church. *(n.p.)*

The sacristy was restored and wooden pews added in 1918. The interior opening of the carved sacristy window is at left center, across from the scalloped entryway into the sanctuary. *(E. C. Kropp Co., Milwaukee)*

THE ALTAR OF SAN JOSE, 2ND. MISSION, SAN ANTONIO, TEX.

The roof of San José's sacristy never collapsed, allowing occasional services to be held there until major repairs were made to the adjoining church. This view shows the sacristy prior to restoration in 1918. *(H. Budow, San Antonio)*

Portal of San Jose (2nd Mission) Built 1718, San Antonio, Texas.

The horizontal crack barely visible above the feet of the
Virgin of Guadalupe over the entrance indicates the
precarious state of the facade by 1900. *(Nic Tengg, San
Antonio, pm. 1909)*

WITTE MUSEUM, SAN ANTONIO, TEXAS

An interior brace to support the endangered facade was constructed by Daughters of the Republic of Texas under the leadership of preservationist Adina De Zavala in 1902. *(Alamo Kodak Finishing Co., San Antonio)*

MISSION SAN JOSÉ DE AGUAYO (SECOND MISSION) BUILT 1720

The original mission convento was transformed by an arched cloister begun by Benedictine priests who came from Pennsylvania in 1859 to rejuvenate San José, but left unfinished when they departed nine years later. *(n.p., pm. 1916)*

Mission San Jose de Acuna (2nd Mission) built 1718, San Antonio, Texas

Admission to San José's church grounds was through the gate at right in the fence, erected by preservationists at the start of the twentieth century to keep farm animals out. *(Albertype Co., Brooklyn)*

RUINS, MISSION SAN JOSE, SAN ANTONIO, TEX.

Walls of San José's unfinished 1860s renovation of the convento into a cloister offered a picturesque spot for photographing tourists. *(n.p.)*

Under the direction of Spanish missionary priests, San José's tower steps were hewn from single blocks of Bois d'Arc wood. *(H. Budow, San Antonio)*

Tower, San Jose Mission.                    SAN ANTONIO, Tex.

Stairs reaching this doorway opened to a vantage point
for this closeup of the original tower, which collapsed in
1928 and was quickly rebuilt. *(Brown News Co.)*

This 1920s aerial view shows San José's roofless church complex plus, across the road toward lower right, the refreshment stand that sold Dr. Pepper—and, at another time, Coca-Cola—to growing numbers of thirsty tourists. *(n.p.)*

San Antono's Fox Photo Co. superimposed a billboard and advertising message over this view to the north of San José's old mission plaza, showing at left center the roofless granary, purchased by the San Antonio Conservation Society and restored by 1933. *(n.p.)*

Federally-funded workers began restoring the mission church in the early years of the Depression but were halted in a question of involvement of church and state, leaving the unfinished dome still open around its sides. *(n.p.)*

With the aid of funds appropriated by the Texas Centennial Commission, the Catholic Church completed the restoration and rededicated the mission church in 1937. *(n.p.)*

New doors by noted Austin woodcarver Peter
Mansbendel duplicated the design of the church's
original Spanish doors, which had disappeared by 1890.
(*n.p.*)

As part of the restoration, landscaping around the unfinished convento-turned-cloister included a garden in the spirit of the one originally on the site. *(n.p.)*

San José's newly-restored dome rises above the cloister arches and beside the also-restored church tower. *(n.p.)*

Reconstruction of San José's small mill, completed in 1938, included this upper room with a millstone, powered below by a wheel turned by water diverted from the mission acequia. *(n.p.)*

Following completion of reconstruction, including perimeter walls with interior rooms for Native American converts, San José was operated as a state park from 1941 until becoming part of San Antonio Missions National Historical Park, formed in 1978. *(n.p.)*

# 5. Mission San Juan Capistrano

The signature feature of Mission San Juan Capistrano is its *espadaña*, the tiered open belfry above its chapel. The mission was founded in East Texas in 1716 and named San José de los Nazonis for a nearby tribe. When reestablished 15 years later beside the San Antonio River, in order to avoid confusion with Mission José upstream it was named for John of Capistrano, a recently-canonized Italian priest who rallied peasants to defeat the Turks at Belgrade in 1456.

The narrow chapel is the mission's major landmark, since the church begun across the mission plaza was never finished. The chapel was reroofed and briefly put back to use in 1877, though a hurricane took the roof off again in 1886. It was reroofed in 1909 and buttressed by federally-funded workers during the Depression of the 1930s.

Like the houses of worship in the other three missions making up San Antonio Missions National Historical Park, San Juan's chapel serves as a Catholic parish church. Several adjoining buildings have been reconstructed.

SAN ANTONIO, Tex. Mission San Juan de Capistran (Third Mission). - Built 1731

This side view of the partly-roofless chapel of Mission San Juan shows the denseness of the undergrowth filling the once-open mission plaza at the beginning of the twentieth century. *(Raphael Tuck & Sons, London)*

Espada Mission, San Antonio, Texas

Though the Missouri publisher confused Espada and San Juan, this early postcard caught the bizarre view of the coffin lid that braced the north window of San Juan's chapel in the late 1890s. *(St. Louis News Co., St. Louis)*

*Mission San Juan Capistran (Third Mission) Built 1716, San Antonio, Tex.*

Most of the interior of San Juan's derelict chapel was unprotected from the elements in the early 1900s, but the rear portion over the altar area remained roofed. *(McLean & Mudge, San Antonio, pm. 1907)*

*Mission San Juan de Capistran. (Third Mission) Built 1716. San Antonio, Texas.*

The five recessed arches of San Juan's chapel, in use by 1756, faced the mission's plaza, here filling up with undergrowth. *(Louis Book Store, San Antonio)*

MISSION SAN JUAN. BUILT 1716
One of the many attractions of San Antonio—on the M. K. & T. Ry.

The Missouri, Kansas and Texas Railway used this view of the rear side of San Juan's chapel to promote travel to San Antonio. *(MK& T Railway)*

Ruins, Espada Mission. San Antonio, Tex.

Overgrown ruins of the old defensive mission plaza wall abutting the southeast corner of the mislabeled San Juan chapel show in this late 1890s postcard view. *(St. Louis News Co., St. Louis)*

Monastery and well of San Juan Capistrano Mission. San Antonio, Texas

The old well and portions of San Juan's convento—since partly restored and serving as a visitor's center—survived at the southwest corner of the mission plaza. *(Grombach-Faisans Co., New Orleans)*

# 6. Mission San Francisco de la Espada

Nearly nine miles down the San Antonio River from the Alamo, Mission Espada is the most remote of the city's five missions. It moved to San Antonio in 1731 from East Texas, where its antecedent was founded in 1690 as the first mission in Spanish Texas. The most familiar feature of its chapel—never permanently replaced by a church—is the irregularly arched door, the subject of much speculation. Was placement of its stones intentional, or did local builders misunderstand instructions on how to make the outer line smooth?

Espada's chapel was preserved in the 1880s by an immigrant French parish priest, Father Francis Bouchu, who rebuilt part of the old convento as his home and conducted services in the chapel until his death in 1907. The nearby irrigation system that carried water from the San Antonio River to mission fields has remained functioning for neighboring farmers for most of the past two and a half-plus centuries, and incorporates the oldest original stone aqueduct still in use in the United States.

SAN ANTONIO. Mission San Francisco de Espada - Built 1730 (The Fourth Mission)

Dispelling the remoteness of Mission Espada's chapel setting seems to be a well-dressed group of tourists, more than the number usually superimposed on scenes—as these are—by noted postcard publisher Raphael Tuck & Sons. *(Raphael Tuck & Sons, London)*

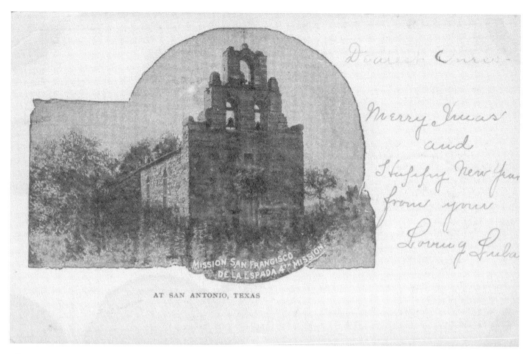

AT SAN ANTONIO, TEXAS

The facade of Mission Espada's chapel was preserved by a parish priest, Father Francis Bouchu, who finished reconstructing the chapel in 1887. *(n.p., pm. 1904)*

Later residents put old structures facing Espada's mission plaza to use, such as the one at far right center, used for a time as the community school. *(Canter & Gut., New York, pm. 1906)*

MISSION SAN FRANCISCO DE LA ESPADA, BUILT 1730
At San Antonio—on the M. K. & T. Ry.

One of Mission Espada's crumbling convento buildings, left center, was roofed to become a general store run by the parish priest, who lived in the refurbished convento building hidden by trees at center. *(MK&T Railway, p.m. 1911)*

19:—MISSION SAN FRANCISCO DE ESPADA, FOURTH MISSION, BUILT 1730, SAN ANTONIO, TEXAS

The second story added in the 1880s to Espada's convento ruins, far left, by Father Bouchu was later removed for reconstruction of a single-story priests' residence adjoining the chapel. *(Hewitt News Service, San Antonio)*

To protect area residents from raiding Comanches, Spanish soldiers added this defensive turret to the mission's walls in the early 1800s. *(n.p., pm. 1914)*

The mid-eighteenth century aqueduct built to carry San Antonio River water over Piedras Creek to irrigate Espada's mission fields has served area farmers ever since. *(George M. Bearce, San Antonio)*

Acequia waters passing the rock walls at this end of Espada's aqueduct provided a sunny spot for doing the family wash, which could be spread out to dry on nearby bushes. *(n.p., p.m. 1911)*

By the end of the 1930s, federal relief workers had spruced up the area around Mission Espada and its chapel, stabilizing surviving rock walls around the mission compound, clearing away underbrush and landscaping with native plants. *(n.p.)*

By the 1930s Espada's chapel appeared virtually as it does today, the broken lines of its doorway arch—Moorish or Visigothic?—still generating speculation as to whether the stones were correctly placed. *(n.p.)*

# 7. The Legacy of Mission Architecture

Though San Antonio's Spanish missions were long closed and even their names were mostly forgotten, the appeal of their ruins as tourist destinations kept them in the forefront of the city's consciousness. At the start of the twentieth century Mission Revival architecture spread eastward from California, through the design of stations by railroads seeking to promote uniqueness for tourists. It found a ready welcome in San Antonio.

The new style arrived at the time of heightened interest in the Alamo—and in the popularity of picture postcards. Design of the Alamo's distinctive curved gable parapet was incorporated in many of the state's Mission Revival designs, causing Mission Revival in Texas to often be called Alamo Revival. San Antonians quickly adopted the style as a favorite in the fast-growing commercial, institutional and residential development of what was then the largest city in Texas. After World War I, Mission / Alamo Revival evolved into Spanish Colonial Revival, also used for many of the landmarks that still define the face of San Antonio.

When Mission Revival burst onto the local scene in 1902 with the Southern Pacific depot, designed by San Francisco architects J. D. Isaacs and D. J. Patterson, an Alamo Revival touch was added with the familiar curve of the gabled parapet atop the Alamo. *(n.p.)*

The depot of the International and Great Northern Railroad, later the Missouri Pacific, was designed in 1907 by San Antonio architect Harvey Page and also used incorporated the Alamo parapet motif into the Mission Revival style. *(H G. Zimmerman & Co., Chicago)*

The Missouri, Kansas and Texas Railroad's Mission Revival style depot, razed in 1968, had twin towers similar to Mission Concepción's, an entrance like Mission San José's and California-style roof gables. *(Albertype Co., Brooklyn)*

Beside the Southern Pacific depot was the appropriately-named Mission Hotel, designed by architect Atlee B. Ayres and restored to become, like the depot, part of the new Sunset Station entertainment complex. *(Joske Bros., San Antonio, pm. 1908)*

An elaborate Mission/Alamo Revival facade adorned the Elks Club building that stood on Avenue E a block from Alamo Plaza. *(S. H. Kress & Co., pm. 1912)*

ST. ANTHONY HOTEL, SAN ANTONIO, TEXAS

Both units of the St. Anthony Hotel, designed by J. Flood Walker on Travis Park, incorporated a strong Alamo Revival motif when first built. The parapets disappeared when a new facade united the hotel as a single structure. *(n.p.)*

Maintaining not just the style but also the sunny ambiance of Spain is evident in the "Old Spanish Effect" of lush plants, fountains and spacious open areas on the St. Anthony Hotel's original roof garden. *(n.p.)*

This fashionable spa in southern San Antonio featured Mission Revival-style towers as well as Alamo-style parapets with flagpoles. *(n.p.)*

The San Antonio Country Club's second clubhouse, completed in 1917, featured an Alamo Revival style red tile roof and gabled parapet on both the main building and the golf caddyhouse at left. *(Albertype Co., Brooklyn)*

The side facade of the Oblate Father's home, overlooking the San Antonio River beside the original St. Mary's Catholic Church, shows a Mission Revival adaptation in ecclesiastical architecture. *(Paul Evers, San Antonio, pm. 1912)*

Fashionable towers and a parapet with an open arch graced the new Bonn Avon School building on Oakland Street, later North St. Mary's Street. *(S. Smith., San Antonio, pm. 1910)*

One of San Antonio's more unusual Mission/Alamo Revival style buildings was this undertaking establishment on part of the site now covered by Rivercenter Mall. *(n.p.)*

When Mission Burial Park opened on lands that once belonged to Mission Concepción, it used Mission/Alamo Revival in renovating a former beef extract factory on the site as this distinctive chapel. *(Dahrooge Co., San Antonio)*

This short-lived beer garden on Maverick Park was dominated by its Alamo Revival parapet, into which was incorporated a vent resembling the shape of the sacristy window at Mission San José. (*Nic Tengg, San Antonio, pm. 1909*)

An Alamo Revival parapet was a cost-effective embellishment when A. W. S. Garden built his military academy near Highland Park. (*H. Budow, San Antonio, pm. 1918*)

Mission Revival residential architecture included the characteristic tile-roofed tower and open balconied area of this home, perhaps famous in 1912 but difficult to identify many years later. *(H. Budow, San Antonio)*

An espadaña with room for three bells, reminiscent of missions San Juan and Espada, topped the facade of the main home of what became the Algo Diferente Guest Ranch northwest of San Antonio. *(n.p., pm. 1932)*

Mission Revival evolved after World War I into the sleeker Spanish Colonial Revival. One of the state's finest buildings in the later style is San Antonio's Municipal Auditorium, opened in 1926. *(n.p.)*

One new Spanish Colonial Revival landmark on San Antonio's expanding skyline of the 1920s was the Plaza Hotel, built beside the San Antonio River in 1927. *(n.p.)*

A late Spanish Colonial Revival highrise landmark, near Municipal Auditorium, is the 1931 Southwestern Bell building, the ornate decoration around its roof eliminated when more stories were added in 1953. *(San Antonio Card Co.)*

Spanish Colonial Revival was chosen for the low "Spanish Village" buildings of Grace Lutheran Sanatorium. *(Artvue Co., New York)*

Spanish Colonial Revival marked the 1922 Mary
Catherine Hall on western San Antonio's Westmoorland
College campus, Trinity University's campus when this
was sent and later Assumption Seminary's. *(n.p., pm. 1951)*

A Spanish Colonial Revival turret and arches adorn Harvey Page's 1925 Taylor Hall, built on the French Place campus occupied then by Saint Mary's Hall and now by San Antonio Academy. *(Artvue Co., New York)*

Spanish Colonial Revival designed by Atlee B. and Robert M. Ayres was chosen as the style for a major expansion of Fort Sam Houston, including this enlisted men's barracks, in the 1930s. *(n.p.)*

The Spanish Colonial Revival centerpiece for the present Randolph Air Force Base is this headquarters bulding, designed by Atlee B. and Robert M. Ayres in 1930. *(Weiner News Co., San Antonio)*

Like San Antonio's MKT depot, Randolph's chapel has towers reminiscent of Mission Concepción and an entrance more like that of Mission San José. *(San Antonio Card Co.)*

As are neighboring buildings at Fort Sam Houston, the longtime Brooke General Hospital was built in the Spanish Colonial Revival style, noted for tile roofs and for Baroque ornamentation concentrated around projecting windows and entrances. *(n.p.)*

Facing Fort Sam Houston's Arthur MacArthur Field is one of the U. S. Army's most distinctive post theaters, transformed from what could be merely a rectangular box with the arches, towers and ornamentation of Spanish Colonial Revival design. *(n.p.)*